If you have any encouragement from being united with Christ, if any comfort from his love, if any fellowship with the Spirit, if any tenderness and compassion, then make my joy complete by being like-minded, having the same love, being one in spirit and purpose. Do nothing out of selfish ambition or vain conceit, but in humility consider others better than yourselves. Each of you should look not only to your own interests, but also to the interests of others. **Your attitude should be the same as that of Christ Jesus: Who, being in very nature God, did not consider equality with God something to be grasped, but made himself nothing, taking the very nature of a servant, being made in human likeness. And being found in appearance as a man, he humbled himself and became obedient to death– even death on a cross!**

Philippians 2:1-8 (Emphasis Added)

Diane Schuessler
KINDLE Operations Coordinator
8608 Poplar Bridge Curve
Bloomington, MN 55437
Office: 952-657-5664
Fax: 952-657-5214
Diane@KINDLEServantLeaders.org

Print copies of the *Cultivating Faith Christ-like Servant Leader Journey* guide for use in fostering and multiplying Christ-like servant leaders is available on Amazon.com.

KINDLE

Fostering & Multiplying
Christ-like Servant Leaders

What is KINDLE?

KINDLE *(Karpenko Institute for Nurturing and Developing Leadership Excellence)* is a non-profit organization formed in 2000. KINDLE's Mission is "to foster and multiply Christ-like servant leaders to enhance the ministry of congregations in their communities and the world."

We hope this mission will resonate with you! We are delighted that you have chosen to invest some of your valuable time and energy in exploring the practices of a Christ-like servant leader. Welcome to this significant journey! We believe that God's Word will transform your life and that your daily pursuit of these practices will shape your understanding of yourself. The more you see yourself as a precious child of God who is a Christ-like servant leader in your areas of influence, the more you can guide others to…

- Celebrate their Baptismal identity (restored, gifted, called);
- Grow more Christ-like, manifesting the grace-filled marks of obedience, well-being, leadership, and community; and
- Foster and multiply generations of Christ-like servant leaders in their congregations, homes, workplaces, communities, and the world.

These three phrases capture KINDLE's definition of a Christ-like servant leader.

As You Begin

This way of seeing yourself may be totally new and somewhat foreign. You may or may not see yourself as a leader, and may never head a committee. Yet whatever you do, you set an example for those closest to you and for others who experience you in your congregation, home, neighborhood, workplace, and beyond. You're in good company with Jesus! He didn't call Himself a leader, either, yet others were drawn to follow the example He set.

The *Christ-like Servant Leader Journey* is not a Bible study. Rather, the *Journey* is a process of listening to God's Word, putting it into practice, and allowing it to shape and form your identity as a Christ-like servant leader.

About Cultivating Faith

Cultivating Faith is one of four strands of practices that KINDLE uses to deepen a person's commitment to Christ-like servant leadership. This strand is composed of five disciplines, or practices:

1. Embrace Sabbath Living
2. Learn and Live Scripture
3. Pray Unceasingly
4. Witness Willingly
5. Serve Others

Much of what we learn comes with practice. We weren't born knowing how to talk, read, walk, play an instrument, or ride a bike, yet someone taught, encouraged, and spurred us on until after a lot of repetition and growth, those practices became second nature. The same is true as we practice Christ-like disciplines. Some of the disciplines may be new for us; others may already be second nature.

KINDLE Christ-like servant leaders practice Christ-like disciplines in the context of community and equip other Christ-like servant leaders to do the same. The beauty of being on the *Journey* with others is that we can encourage and spur one another on and celebrate what God is doing as He transforms us, a step at a time over time. Along the way, we begin to discover the thoughts, practices, and heart of Christ-like servant leaders have become part of who we are.

It is our prayer that during these 8 weeks, you'll be amazed and enlivened by the difference this *Journey* experience makes, and that you'll lead others into this way of life too.

Getting the Most Out of the Christ-like Servant Leader Journey

Week 1 includes a brief, simple self-assessment of the five Christ-like servant leader practices for Cultivating Faith and guides you in creating a personal growth plan related to the knowledge, skill, or attitude of one of the five practices.

Each week, the *Christ-like Servant Leader Journey* has a distinct rhythm …

- **Preview Page**
  This page calls us to **Remember Who We Are** as Christ-like servant leaders and provides a roadmap for the week with the **Week's Focus**, **Core Concept**, and **Personal Growth Plan** (see page 10). You'll also identify a **SMART Objective** that supports progress on your personal growth plan. A **Daily Prayer** will shape your Christ-like servant leader living throughout the week.

- **Daily Scripture Reflection**
  Each day, you'll read a portion of God's Word and make note of the main thought. As you read, listen for the "still small voice" of God's leading in the context of one of the Christ-like servant leader practices. Read again, pause, and consider what God is saying to you and what you'll do about it.

- **Prayers**
  How does the Scripture move you to pray? In praise and thanks? With apology, asking forgiveness and help? For wisdom or some other need? Know your Heavenly Father loves to have you come just as you are, with whatever is on your heart and mind.

- **Christ-like Servant Leader Cluster Meeting**
  This 1-hour weekly meeting provides the opportunity and privilege of gathering with other growing Christ-like servant leaders for support, encouragement, and accountability. You'll each share what God has been showing you and what you're doing about it. In the process, you'll become enlivened for the coming week. You'll also share the gift of prayer support.

A Final Word

We're each so uniquely designed by our Creator. Our life experiences and relationships are unique as well. That includes our faith journeys! No two are alike. As we come together on this *Christ-like Servant Leader Journey*, we become tour guides for each other. Some have traveled the path before and will provide support and encouragement to you. For others, you will be that more experienced guide providing direction to them. In time, you may even come to realize you can invite others into the *Journey* with a cluster of your own!

Our Journey Begins...

Ask a volunteer to read the opening prayer:

Jesus, I am overwhelmed by Your grace in my life. As I reflect on Your transforming power, give me the opportunity and the ability to testify to that power in my life so that it might touch others in a profound and God-pleasing way. Amen.

– Kindling the Heart of the Christ-like Servant Leader, 3rd Edition (page 4)

1. Share one of your favorite Bible passages. Why is it special to you?

2. As you reflect back on the challenges of your own life, what "things" have helped "get you through them?"

3. Ask a volunteer to read the passage below.
   But blessed is the man who trusts me, God,
   *   the woman who sticks with God.*
   They're like trees replanted in Eden,
   *   putting down roots near the rivers—*
   Never a worry through the hottest of summers,
   *   never dropping a leaf,*
   Serene and calm through droughts,
   *   bearing fresh fruit every season. – Jeremiah 17:7-8 (The Message)*

   What catches your attention in this reading, and why?

4. What's one hope you have for this cluster during the next seven weeks?

5. ***Cluster leader reads:*** Have you ever been encouraged and equipped to set a personal growth plan that helps you put down roots near the river? You may be regular in worship, but haven't really activated your relationship with God, not knowing where to start. Or perhaps you've been a lifelong Christ-follower, but your faith life has become somewhat status quo. You may even desire more of God, but don't know the next step.

   You'll discover that KINDLE's Cultivating Faith practices provide the structure to help you put down roots near the river. Each Christ-like Servant Leader Journey Guide is a unique opportunity to develop a personal growth plan related to one of the five practices. Can you imagine moving from "someday, I'll…" to actually growing closer to Jesus in just 8 weeks? That's the power of a personal growth plan. Pages 4-9 will get you started.

6. If you've used the *Cultivating Faith Journey Guide* before, what growth plan did you set, and what resulted?

Developing a Personal Growth Plan

Step 1: Self-Assess Strengths and Weaknesses

Below is a brief, simple self-assessment of the Christ-like servant leader practices for *Cultivating Faith*. In this step, read only the description of each practice in bold italic and rate the frequency to which you engage in it using the scale:

1	2	3	4	5	6	7	8
Very Infrequently		*Somewhat Infrequently*		*Somewhat Frequently*		*Very Frequently*	

Remember, this is for your personal use and provides a "snapshot" of your development as a Christ-like servant leader at this point in time. We **all** have strengths and weaknesses. We never fully arrive!

PRACTICE 1.1 EMBRACE SABBATH LIVING

RATING

Eagerly worship, partake in Holy Communion, and nurture additional behaviors which foster spiritual renewal and rest.

OUTCOMES

1.1 Knowledge — Understand the Biblical meaning and rhythm of Sabbath living.

1.1 Skill — Be fully present before the Triune God by cultivating Sabbath living behaviors day by day.

1.1 Attitude — Realize that cultivating Sabbath living behaviors that refresh and renew is a lifelong, daily discipline.

PRACTICE 1.2 LEARN AND LIVE SCRIPTURE

RATING

Discover and apply the truths of Scripture in all your comings and goings.

OUTCOMES

1.2 Knowledge — Acknowledge the role of Scripture in transforming and renewing the Christ-like servant leader.

1.2 Skill — Reflect on Scripture, discern its truths, and apply them to daily life.

1.2 Attitude — Display a willingness to be formed as a Christ-like servant leader through interaction with Scripture.

PRACTICE 1.3 PRAY UNCEASINGLY

RATING

Pray continually – alone and with others – for all people, the church, and the world.

OUTCOMES

1.3 Knowledge — Understand how God uses private and corporate prayer in forming the Christ-like servant leader.

1.3 Skill — Demonstrate an ability to pray alone and with others.

1.3 Attitude — Cherish prayer as a means to respond to God's Word, discern His heart, and grasp His purpose.

PRACTICE 1.4 WITNESS WILLINGLY

RATING

Accept God's call to be a voice and example of His restoring grace and mercy in your communities and in the world.

OUTCOMES

1.4 Knowledge — Discover how the Gospel of Jesus compels a Christ-like servant leader to witness in word and deed.

1.4 Skill — Live in a manner that gives witness to Jesus Christ as your Savior and Lord.

1.4 Attitude — Be willing to share what God is doing for, through, and around you.

PRACTICE 1.5 SERVE OTHERS

RATING

Go forth as a living sacrifice, being God's ambassador of reconciliation to all people, especially to the least of these.

OUTCOMES

1.5 Knowledge — Recognize that serving others is part of God's restoring and reconciling work in the world.

1.5 Skill — Serve others by practicing hospitality, showing mercy, and doing justice.

1.5 Attitude — Open your heart generously, as Jesus did, when you serve others.

Step 2: Identify Christ's Gracious Invitation

1. Identify **one** practice in which God is inviting you to grow and to enhance your capacities as a Christ-like servant leader. You may have assessed it anywhere from 1-8. The key is to focus only on the one practice in which God is inviting you to grow.

2. Read through the outcomes (Knowledge, Skill, Attitude) for the one practice you have chosen.

3. Put an "X" by the **one outcome** you will focus on in this growth plan.

Congratulations! You've just completed a key step in growing as a Christ-like servant leader! When you put things in writing for a purpose, the potential for reaching a goal goes up!

Step 3: Developing Your Personal Growth Plan

Based upon the **outcome** you identified in Step 2, begin to define **SMART** objectives that can help you grow and mature as a Christ-like servant leader. Use the form on page 6 to create your personal growth plan. *Check out some sample growth plans on pages 7-9 for ideas.*

Closing

Let's take a quick look at what's coming up this week, starting on page 10. Each week, there is a preview of focus for the coming week as we prepare for our next time together. There are daily readings for the first five days, and then a chance to reflect on all those readings in a more focused way on day 6. You'll also preview our next meeting on day 6 so you can be ready to discuss the questions together.

How can we pray for you this week?

Write down any prayer requests below and include them as you close in prayer:

Praying in Your Cluster

If praying with others is new to you, the best way to learn to pray silently or aloud is to just try it. KINDLE clusters provide an ideal size and appreciative community in which to grow in praying for one another. It's often easier to pray for another's needs than for our own, plus we bless people when we ask God to be at work in their lives. Suggested guidelines for group prayer are:

1. Keep it simple, keep it short.
2. Pray from the heart.
3. God is listening. Trust Him.
4. Our own words are OK.

Parents teach their children to say "please", "thank you", "I'm sorry." Those are great phrases when learning to pray, too! In a small cluster, praying for the person on your right can be an easy approach. Give it a try:

Lord Jesus, thank you for … *(one aspect of your cluster experience today.)*
Please help / guide / encourage *(name)* this week as he/she *(prayer request noted above.)*

My Personal Growth Plan

1. Christ-like servant leader practice: _____

2. Specific outcome selected for this growth plan: _____
   _____

3. Reason for choosing this outcome: _____
   _____

Write SMART Objectives that are:

- **S**pecific
- **M**easurable
- **A**ttainable
- **R**ealistic
- **T**ime Bound

4. SMART Objectives

   a. _____
      _____
      _____

   b. _____
      _____
      _____

   c. _____
      _____
      _____

5. Resources needed to meet my objectives …

6. How can your cluster group help you achieve your objectives?

7. How will you know you've achieved your objectives? What will that feel or look like?

KINDLE *Personal Growth Plan Examples: Knowledge*

Christ-like servant leader practice: Embrace Sabbath Living

Specific outcome: Knowledge – Understand the Biblical meaning and rhythm of Sabbath Living.

Reason for selecting this outcome: I want to more fully understand "Sabbath" and Sabbath living, hoping that leads to new skills and attitudes as well.

SMART Objectives:
    a. Daily invite the Holy Spirit to provide insight that moves me to practice Sabbath living.
    b. Read *Sabbath Living* by Wayne Mueller in the next six weeks.
    c. Make a list of new discoveries and ways to experiment!
    d. Commit to pursue several behaviors that will help me embrace Sabbath living.

Resources Needed to Meet Objectives: The book *Sabbath Living*, by Wayne Mueller

How can your Cluster help you achieve your objectives: Prayers and weekly check in.

How will you know when you've achieved your objectives: Book finished. Have identified and am embracing at least three ways I can daily refresh and renew.

Christ-like servant leader practice: Learn and Live Scriptures

Specific outcome: Knowledge – Acknowledge the role of Scripture in transforming and renewing the Christ-like servant leader.

Reason for selecting this outcome: I haven't read the Bible at all, so this is a good place to start.

SMART Objectives:
    a. Invest time daily to read and consider the Christ-like Servant Leader Journey Guide readings.
    b. Meet with my cluster weekly.
    c. Read context and look for background when I have questions about the meaning of verses.

Resources Needed to Meet Objectives: The Christ-like Servant Leader Journey Guide for "Cultivating Faith" and a Bible. People who can guide me into truth.

How can your Cluster help you achieve your objectives: Prayers and help with questions.

How will you know when you've achieved your objectives: If Scripture is transforming and renewing, I expect my life will be different as a husband, father, and business owner.

Suggested Reading List:
- *Sabbath: Finding Rest, Renewal, and Delight in Our Busy Lives*, Wayne Mueller, Bantam Books, c. 1999.
- *The Story, NIV: The Bible as One Continuing Story of God and His People*, Max Lucado and Randy Frazee, Zondervan Publishing, c. 2011.
- *Made to Pray*, Chris Heinz, Westbow Press, c. 2014.
- *God Space – Where Spiritual Conversations Happen Naturally*, Doug Pollock, Group Publishing, Loveland, CO, c. 2009.
- *Joining Jesus on His Mission, How To Be an Everyday Missionary*, Greg Finke, c. 2014, www.tenthpowerpublishing.com.

Christ-like servant leader practice: Pray Unceasingly

Specific outcome: Skill – demonstrate an ability and comfortableness in praying alone and with others.

Reason for selecting this outcome: This is new territory for me and something I feel led to learn.

SMART Objectives:
    a. Use BibleGateway.com to print a list of where "pray" is used in Paul's letters.
    b. Read at least one verse about prayer each day and journal about what I learn.
    c. Consider at least three of the prayers Paul prayed for believers each week, and make a list of what he included in his prayers. Ask God to use this to shape my prayers.
    d. Ask a staff member who demonstrates the ability to pray with others instruct me in how to do this.
    e. Pray with my cluster each week.

Resources Needed to Meet Objectives: The Bible.

How can your Cluster help you achieve your objectives: Praying together and a chance to share what I'm learning.

How will you know when you've achieved your objectives: I will be more comfortable and confident when asked to pray or praying with others.

Christ-like servant leader practice: Serve Others

Specific outcome: Skill - Serve others by practicing hospitality, showing mercy, and doing justice.

Reason for selecting this outcome: There's a widow living next door who just got home from the hospital who may need some help.

SMART Objectives:
    a. Stop by with flowers this weekend and see how she's doing.
    b. Ask if she has any needs that I could address.
    c. After my visit, prayerfully identify which needs I can meet and where I need to invite others to help.
    d. If others are needed, ask our Parish Nurse to help resource me, and begin to make those connections.
    e. Continue to pray for her healing and well-being.

Resources Needed to Meet Objectives: Possibly church or community resources. Will know more once I ask.

How can your Cluster help you achieve your objectives: Encourage, resource, and help as needs arise.

How will you know when you've achieved your objectives: My neighbor's needs will be filled.

Christ-like servant leader practice: Embrace Sabbath Living

Specific outcome: Attitude – Realize that cultivating Sabbath living behaviors that refresh and renew is a lifelong, daily discipline.

Reason for selecting this outcome: I know that cultivating an attitude of thankfulness impacts my day and I've gotten off track lately.

SMART Objectives:
    a. Keep a gratitude journal, identifying 5 things to thank God for each day. Try not to repeat!
    b. Include prayers of thanksgiving with my family at our evening meal.
    c. Share my journal with 3 other people each week and discuss God's blessings.
    d. This week: Get rid of old, negative CDs.
    e. Listen to praise music whenever I'm in the car and at home, too.

Resources Needed to Meet Objectives: Notebook. Christian music CDs.

How can your Cluster help you achieve your objectives: Prayers and weekly check in.

How will you know when you've achieved your objectives: I'll be more aware God is with me and give thanks instead of complaining or wanting what I don't have. I think it will impact our family culture, too.

Christ-like servant leader practice: Witness Willingly

Specific outcome: Attitude – Be willing to share what God is doing for, through, and around you.

Reason for selecting this outcome: I have a wide network of non-Christian friends and am fearful of talking to them about God.

SMART Objectives:
    a. Read God Space within the next 6 weeks to become better equipped and encouraged.
    b. Make a list of 5 people that I want to pray for each week and pray daily.
    c. Try mentioning God during conversations when we're face-to-face.
    d. Post verses and praises that speak to me on Facebook weekly. Tell everyone what he's done and is doing!
    e. Talk more with Christians about faith and God one or more times a week. Practice makes perfect – or at least makes it easier to talk about God.

Resources Needed to Meet Objectives: The book *God Space*, by Doug Pollock.

How can your Cluster help you achieve your objectives: Prayers and weekly check in.

How will you know when you've achieved your objectives: I'll be more comfortable talking with my non-Christian friends about God.

Cultivating Faith: Five Foundational Practices
Daily Reflections from God's Word for Week 2

Remembering Who We Are

A KINDLE Christ-like servant leader helps others:

- Celebrate their Baptismal identity (restored, gifted, called);
- Grow more Christ-like, manifesting the Grace-Filled Marks of obedience, well-being, leadership, and community; and
- Foster and multiply generations of Christ-like servant leaders in their congregations, homes, workplaces, communities, and the world.

This Week's Focus: Overview of the Practices in Cultivating Faith

KINDLE Christ-like servant leaders are maturing as they practice Christ-like disciplines in the context of community and equip other Christ-like servant leaders to do the same.

Core Concept

God shapes and forms us as we make these five foundational practices part of our everyday life:

- Embrace Sabbath Living
- Learn and Live Scripture
- Pray Unceasingly
- Witness Willingly
- Serve Others

Now What?

Begin where you are, experienced in these practices or not. It's always about the next doable step and the power of incremental change over the long haul. It's realizing growing as a Christ-like servant leader is much more a marathon than a sprint. This week, allow God to speak into your life and see what happens!

Personal Growth Plan

Complete the draft of your *Growth Plan* on page 6. Which SMART objective will you begin to pursue this week?

_____

_____

_____

For Daily Prayer

Jesus, Your example of servant leadership is so powerful. Today I need Your grace and Your Spirit's help to live and lead as You would. I ask that You send the Comforter, as you promised, to give me the courage and understanding to reflect You this day. In Your name. Amen.

– Kindling the Heart of the Christ-like Servant Leader, 3rd Edition (page 39)

Daily Bible Reflections: Day 1

Date: __ / __ / __

Read and Highlight: Romans 12:1-2 (An example for you to consider...)

Words or phrases that catch my attention:

urge, God's mercy, offer, living sacrifices, holy, pleasing, spiritual worship, do not conform, be transformed, renewing of mind, test and approve

Major Thought:

God's mercy calls us to a new standard - to offer and align our lives to what pleases God, not our culture. Our lives are transformed in an ongoing way as we renew our minds in God's truth and grace.

What impresses me the most, and what I'll do about it:

The word 'urge' flags this as a heartfelt plea to live aware of God's mercy and to freely offer myself to what pleases God. I don't always live a life pleasing to God, so I need to listen to God's Word and let it reshape my living daily. This week, I'll determine to find a time in which I can be consistent.

What does this Scripture lead me to pray about? (This may be praise and thanks; or with apology, asking forgiveness and help; or a request for wisdom, or for some other need.)

Thank you for your boundless mercies, Lord. They're new every morning! I offer myself to You this day, and ask your help in setting a time I can consistently let your Word speak into my life. When I'm tempted, give me courage to do what's right.

Daily Bible Reflections: Day 2

Date: __ / __ / __

Read and Highlight: 2 Timothy 3:10-17

Words or phrases that catch my attention:

_____

_____

_____

Major Thought:

_____

_____

What impresses me the most, and what I'll do about it:

_____

_____

_____

What does this Scripture lead me to pray about?

_____

_____

Daily Bible Reflections: Day 3

Read and Highlight: Matthew 6:5-15

Words or phrases that catch my attention:

_____

_____

_____

Major Thought:

_____

What impresses me the most, and what I'll do about it:

_____

_____

_____

What does this Scripture lead me to pray about?

_____

_____

Daily Bible Reflections: Day 4

Date: ___ /___ /___

Read and Highlight: 2 Corinthians 5:11-21

Words or phrases that catch my attention:

_____

_____

_____

Major Thought:

_____

What impresses me the most, and what I'll do about it:

_____

_____

_____

What does this Scripture lead me to pray about?

_____

_____

Daily Bible Reflections: Day 5

Date: ___ /___ /___

Read and Highlight: John 13:12-17

Words or phrases that catch my attention:

_____
_____
_____

Major Thought:

_____

What impresses me the most, and what I'll do about it:

_____
_____
_____

What does this Scripture lead me to pray about?

_____
_____

Daily Bible Reflections: Day 6

Date: ___ /___ /___

Review the passages you reflected on this week.

Which reading(s) spoke most directly to you this week?

_____
_____
_____

What is God saying to you in this reading?

_____
_____
_____

How are you responding?

_____
_____
_____

*Prepare for The Christ-like Servant Leader Cluster Meeting by
reviewing the Agenda on the next page and considering your responses.*

Opening Prayer (invite someone to read)

Lord Jesus, thank you for claiming us as your beloved children in the waters of Baptism and for filling us with your Spirit of truth. As we gather in your name, let your Word speak through each one of us in ways that shape, inspire, and encourage us on this journey of seeing ourselves and living as Christ-like servant leaders. Amen.

Discussion Questions

1. How did you experience "God's presence" in a special way this week?

2. Which of the five Scripture readings this week has been particularly meaningful to you? What has God been saying to you through it? How are you responding?

3. What good thing could you do this week? Who can you bless? (Think about people in your congregation, home, workplace, neighborhood, and community.)

4. Share the rough draft of your Growth Plan with your cluster. What is the SMART objective you began to address this week? How did it go?

Closing Prayer

Let's take time to do two things:

1. Write down prayer requests:
   a. As we pray for each other this week, what is one thing can we pray for you?

   b. As we learn and live out the practices that cultivate faith, what are we led to pray?

2. Pray together, focusing on the needs identified in number 1.

Embrace Sabbath Living
Daily Reflections from God's Word for Week 3

Remembering Who We Are

A KINDLE Christ-like servant leader helps others:

- Celebrate their Baptismal identity (restored, gifted, called);
- Grow more Christ-like, manifesting the Grace-Filled Marks of obedience, well-being, leadership, and community; and
- Foster and multiply generations of Christ-like servant leaders in their congregations, homes, workplaces, communities, and the world.

This Week's Focus: Practice 1.1 — Embrace Sabbath Living

Eagerly worship, partake in Holy Communion, and nurture additional behaviors which foster spiritual renewal and rest.

- *Knowledge — Understand the Biblical meaning and rhythm of Sabbath living.*
- *Skill — Be fully present before the Triune God by cultivating Sabbath living behaviors day by day.*
- *Attitude — Realize that cultivating Sabbath living behaviors that refresh and renew is a lifelong, daily discipline.*

Core Concept

Christ-like servant leaders seek regular opportunities to join other believers in worship as well as pursue various behaviors that offer spiritual refreshment, renewal, and rest.

Now What?

The word "Sabbath" means stop, cease, rest, pause. What drives our busyness and lack of rest? How does that impact relationships? As the Scriptures speak, notice the reasons God gives for the command and why Sabbath living matters. Begin to consider what you might stop doing in order to pause and what you'd intentionally do to refresh. You might check out SabbathManifesto.org for thought starters.

Personal Growth Plan

Which **SMART Objective(s)** are you pursuing this week?

_____

_____

_____

For Daily Prayer

Gracious Heavenly Father, I long to rest in You. I yearn to be renewed by Your hand. Open my heart to the ways You want to refresh me. Help me make space in my life for rest in You. In Jesus' name. Amen.

– Kindling the Heart of the Christ-like Servant Leader, 3rd Edition (page 1)

Daily Bible Reflections: Day 1

Read and Highlight: Genesis 2:2-3

Words or phrases that catch my attention:

_____

_____

_____

Major Thought:

_____

What impresses me the most, and what I'll do about it:

_____

_____

_____

What does this Scripture lead me to pray about? (This may be praise and thanks; or with apology, asking forgiveness and help; or a request for wisdom, or for some other need.)

_____

_____

Daily Bible Reflections: Day 2

Read and Highlight: Exodus 20:8-11

Words or phrases that catch my attention:

_____

_____

_____

Major Thought:

_____

What impresses me the most, and what I'll do about it:

_____

_____

_____

What does this Scripture lead me to pray about?

_____

_____

Daily Bible Reflections: Day 3

Date: ___ / ___ / ___

Read and Highlight: Deuteronomy 5:12-15

Words or phrases that catch my attention:

_____

_____

_____

Major Thought:

_____

What impresses me the most, and what I'll do about it:

_____

_____

_____

What does this Scripture lead me to pray about?

_____

_____

Daily Bible Reflections: Day 4

Date: ___ / ___ / ___

Read and Highlight: Psalm 95:1-7

Words or phrases that catch my attention:

_____

_____

_____

Major Thought:

_____

What impresses me the most, and what I'll do about it:

_____

_____

_____

What does this Scripture lead me to pray about?

_____

_____

Daily Bible Reflections: Day 5

Read and Highlight: 1 Corinthians 11:23-30

Words or phrases that catch my attention:

_____

_____

_____

Major Thought:

_____

What impresses me the most, and what I'll do about it:

_____

_____

_____

What does this Scripture lead me to pray about?

_____

_____

Daily Bible Reflections: Day 6

Date: __ / __ / __

Review the passages you reflected on this week.

Which reading(s) spoke most directly to you this week?

_____

_____

_____

What is God saying to you in this reading?

_____

_____

_____

How are you responding?

_____

_____

_____

*Prepare for The Christ-like Servant Leader Cluster Meeting by
reviewing the Agenda on the next page and considering your responses.*

Christ-like Servant Leader Cluster Meeting 3

Opening Prayer

Pray together, or ask for a volunteer to pray the following prayer:

Creator God, You designed us to need times of rest and refreshment, and you set the example for us to follow. If we're honest, we know we do much better embracing busyness than embracing Sabbath living! We ask you to guide our time and provide the insight, refreshment, and encouragement we need to rest and delight in you. In your name we pray, Amen.

Discussion Questions:

1. What drives our busyness and lack of rest? How does that impact relationships and our worship life?

2. Which of the five Scripture readings this week has been particularly meaningful to you? What has God been saying to you through it? How are you responding?

3. How might Sabbath living affect your ability to be a Christ-like servant leader in your congregation, home, neighborhood, or workplace?

4. Who in your family, neighborhood, or workplace needs the gift of your time this week? What shape might it take?

5. What **SMART Objective** did you pursue this week related to your growth plan? What went well? Any challenges or roadblocks?

Closing Prayer

Let's take time to do two things:

1. Write down prayer requests:
   a. As we pray for each other this week, what is one thing can we pray for you?

   b. As we learn and live out the practice *Embrace Sabbath Living*, what are we led to pray?

2. Pray together, focusing on the needs identified in number 1.

Learn and Live Scripture
Daily Reflections from God's Word for Week 4

Remembering Who We Are

A KINDLE Christ-like servant leader helps others:

- Celebrate their Baptismal identity (restored, gifted, called);
- Grow more Christ-like, manifesting the Grace-Filled Marks of obedience, well-being, leadership, and community; and
- Foster and multiply generations of Christ-like servant leaders in their congregations, homes, workplaces, communities, and the world.

This Week's Focus: Practice 1.2 — Learn and Live Scripture

Discover and apply the truths of Scripture in all your comings and goings.

- *Knowledge — Acknowledge the role of Scripture in transforming and renewing the Christ-like servant leader.*
- *Skill — Reflect on Scripture, discern its truths, and apply them to daily life.*
- *Attitude — Display a willingness to be formed as a Christ-like servant leader through interaction with Scripture.*

Core Concept

In Baptism, we're united with Christ. His name and identity are placed on us! God has given us the gift of Scripture and calls us to put its grace and truth into practice, letting it shape and form our living as Christ-like servant leaders.

Now What?

As you interact with the readings this week, pay special attention to the blessings that come as we *Learn and Live Scripture*. Be thinking about how learning and living Scripture compares to a life that learns and lives our culture's values.

Personal Growth Plan

Which **SMART objective(s)** will you pursue this week?

_____

_____

_____

For Daily Prayer

Jesus, You are the transforming Word of God. As I come to You today, prompt me to take Your Word into my heart and mind as I live in its Truth. How I love Your Word—thank You. Amen.

– Kindling the Heart of the Christ-like Servant Leader, 3rd Edition (page 2)

Daily Bible Reflections: Day 1

Read and Highlight: Matthew 7:24-27

Words or phrases that catch my attention:

_____

_____

_____

Major Thought:

_____

What impresses me the most, and what I'll do about it:

_____

_____

_____

What does this Scripture lead me to pray about? (This may be praise and thanks; or with apology, asking forgiveness and help; or a request for wisdom, or for some other need.)

_____

_____

Daily Bible Reflections: Day 2

Date: ___ /___ /___

Read and Highlight: John 1:1-5, 14-18

Words or phrases that catch my attention:

_____

_____

_____

Major Thought:

_____

What impresses me the most, and what I'll do about it:

_____

_____

_____

What does this Scripture lead me to pray about?

_____

_____

Daily Bible Reflections: Day 3

Date: ___ /___ /___

Read and Highlight: Ephesians 6:10-17

Words or phrases that catch my attention:

_____
_____
_____

Major Thought:

_____

What impresses me the most, and what I'll do about it:

_____
_____
_____

What does this Scripture lead me to pray about?

_____
_____

Daily Bible Reflections: Day 4

Date: ___ /___ /___

Read and Highlight: Hebrews 5:11-14

Words or phrases that catch my attention:

_____
_____
_____

Major Thought:

_____

What impresses me the most, and what I'll do about it:

_____
_____
_____

What does this Scripture lead me to pray about?

_____
_____

Daily Bible Reflections: Day 5

Read and Highlight: John 15:1-4, 7-11

Words or phrases that catch my attention:

_____

_____

_____

Major Thought:

_____

What impresses me the most, and what I'll do about it:

_____

_____

_____

What does this Scripture lead me to pray about?

_____

_____

Daily Bible Reflections: Day 6

Review the passages you reflected on this week.

Which reading(s) spoke most directly to you this week?

_____

_____

_____

What is God saying to you in this reading?

_____

_____

_____

How are you responding?

_____

_____

_____

***Prepare for The Christ-like Servant Leader Cluster Meeting by
reviewing the Agenda on the next page and considering your responses.***

Opening Prayer

Pray together, or ask for a volunteer to pray the following prayer:

Lord Jesus, Your words are full of grace and truth, life and light! What delightful discoveries You are providing! Create in us a hunger to *Learn and Live Scripture* so Your words take root in us and shape our living as Christ-like servant leaders. Thank You for loving us. Amen.

Discussion Questions:

1. What value did your family place on the Bible as you were growing up?

2. Which of the five Scripture readings this week has been particularly meaningful to you? What has God been saying to you through it? How are you responding?

3. What strength does learning and living Scripture build into a Christ-like servant leader's living? How does this life in Christ compare with the culture around you?

4. Who in your network doesn't yet know Jesus, but does need to experience His love? In what ways can they experience it through you?

5. What **SMART Objective** did you address in your growth plan this week? What went well? Did any roadblocks arise?

Closing Prayer

Let's take time to do two things:

1. Write down prayer requests:
   a. As we pray for each other this week, what is one thing can we pray for you?

   b. As we learn and live out the practice *Learn and Live Scripture*, what are we led to pray?

2. Pray together, focusing on the needs identified in number 1.

Pray Unceasingly
Daily Reflections from God's Word for Week 5

Remembering Who We Are

A KINDLE Christ-like servant leader helps others:

- Celebrate their Baptismal identity (restored, gifted, called);
- Grow more Christ-like, manifesting the Grace-Filled Marks of obedience, well-being, leadership, and community; and
- Foster and multiply generations of Christ-like servant leaders in their congregations, homes, workplaces, communities, and the world.

This Week's Focus: Practice 1.3 — Pray Unceasingly

Pray continually – alone and with others – for all people, the church, and the world.
- *Knowledge — Understand how God uses private and corporate prayer in forming the Christ-like servant leader.*
- *Skill — Demonstrate an ability to pray alone and with others.*
- *Attitude — Cherish prayer as a means to respond to God's Word, discern His heart, and grasp His purpose.*

Core Concept

Jesus prayed as part of His intimate union with His Father and only did what He saw his Father doing (John 5:19). United with Christ in Baptism, God invites us into that same intimacy. As we lead our lives as Christ-like servant leaders, we have many fears and needs. What a perfect place to be! Fears and needs turn our heart to the One who reminds us how deeply we're loved and forgiven and Who is eager to guide, supply, and empower our living.

Now What?

Watch the way in which young children love to whisper into a parent's ear or who they run to when they're hurt or have a need and the parent's responsiveness. Consider yourself as that child turning to your Father in heaven whose heart is towards you! As you listen to the Scriptures, pay special attention to what He's eager to provide.

Personal Growth Plan

Which **SMART objective(s)** will you pursue this week?

_____

_____

_____

For Daily Prayer

Dear Jesus, thank You for desiring a relationship with me. Since You are the most important relationship in my life, forgive me for the times I could have spent with You, but did not. Create in me the kind of eagerness for prayer that pleases You. Amen.

– Kindling the Heart of the Christ-like Servant Leader, 3rd Edition (page 3)

Daily Bible Reflections: Day 1

Date: __ / __ / __

Read and Highlight: 1 Timothy 2:1-7

Words or phrases that catch my attention:

_____

_____

_____

Major Thought:

_____

What impresses me the most, and what I'll do about it:

_____

_____

_____

What does this Scripture lead me to pray about? (This may be praise and thanks; or with apology, asking forgiveness and help; or a request for wisdom, or for some other need.)

_____

_____

Daily Bible Reflections: Day 2

Date: __ / __ / __

Read and Highlight: Psalm 42

Words or phrases that catch my attention:

_____

_____

_____

Major Thought:

_____

What impresses me the most, and what I'll do about it:

_____

_____

_____

What does this Scripture lead me to pray about?

_____

_____

Daily Bible Reflections: Day 3

Date: ___ /___ /___

Read and Highlight: Luke 11:1-13

Words or phrases that catch my attention:

_____

_____

_____

Major Thought:

_____

What impresses me the most, and what I'll do about it:

_____

_____

_____

What does this Scripture lead me to pray about?

_____

_____

Daily Bible Reflections: Day 4

Date: ___ /___ /___

Read and Highlight: Philippians 4:4-9

Words or phrases that catch my attention:

_____

_____

_____

Major Thought:

_____

What impresses me the most, and what I'll do about it:

_____

_____

_____

What does this Scripture lead me to pray about?

_____

_____

Daily Bible Reflections: Day 5

Read and Highlight: Hebrews 4:14–16

Words or phrases that catch my attention:

_____
_____
_____

Major Thought:

_____

What impresses me the most, and what I'll do about it:

_____
_____
_____

What does this Scripture lead me to pray about?

_____
_____

Daily Bible Reflections: Day 6

Date: ___ /___ /___

Review the passages you reflected on this week.

Which reading(s) spoke most directly to you this week?

_____
_____
_____

What is God saying to you in this reading?

_____
_____
_____

How are you responding?

_____
_____
_____

Prepare for The Christ-like Servant Leader Cluster Meeting by reviewing the Agenda on the next page and considering your responses.

Christ-like Servant Leader Cluster Meeting 5   Date: __ / __ / __

Opening Prayer

Pray together, or ask for a volunteer to pray the following prayer:

Ever-present Holy Spirit, stir our hearts and minds to know the gift of prayer more fully. Give us a spirit of freedom in bringing who we are, with all our fears and concerns, to the One who deeply loves and forgives us and can help. In Jesus' name. Amen.

Discussion Questions:

1. What's been your view and practice of prayer so far? (This is a judgement free zone. Growth always begins where we are... and we're never where we imagine we want to be! Prayer isn't about "doing it right". It's about being who we are with God.)

2. Which of the five Scripture readings this week has been particularly meaningful to you? What has God been saying to you through it? How are you responding?

3. What is God eager to provide as Christ-like servant leaders pray unceasingly? How might this practice take shape in ways that help others realize the gift of prayer?

4. Who's "standing in the need of prayer" that you can intercede for (pray on behalf of) this week?

5. What **SMART Objective** did you move towards in your growth plan this week? What more in your plan do you still hope to pursue?

Closing Prayer

Let's take time to do two things:

1. Write down prayer requests:
   a. As we pray for each other this week, what is one thing can we pray for you?

   b. As we learn and live out the practice *Pray Unceasingly*, what are we led to pray?

2. Pray together, focusing on the needs identified in number 1.

Witness Willingly
Daily Reflections from God's Word for Week 6

Remembering Who We Are

A KINDLE Christ-like servant leader helps others:

- Celebrate their Baptismal identity (restored, gifted, called);
- Grow more Christ-like, manifesting the Grace-Filled Marks of obedience, well-being, leadership, and community; and
- Foster and multiply generations of Christ-like servant leaders in their congregations, homes, workplaces, communities, and the world.

This Week's Focus: Practice 1.4 — Witness Willingly

Accept God's call to be a voice and example of His restoring grace and mercy in your communities and in the world.

- *Knowledge — Discover how the Gospel of Jesus compels a Christ-like servant leader to witness in word and deed.*
- *Skill — Live in a manner that gives witness to Jesus Christ as your Savior and Lord.*
- *Attitude — Be willing to share what God is doing for, through, and around you.*

Core Concept

Christ-like servant leaders embody Jesus' mission as they demonstrate God's love in action and are always ready to share how the Good News of God's mercy and grace is at work in their lives each day.

Now What?

We can only give witness to what we've seen and heard. As you engage the daily readings, consider them as God's playbook for life in Christ. See what you discover about God, about yourself, and about those far from God. How do the daily discoveries empower and shape your daily witness? In what ways can you be a voice and example of God's restoring grace and mercy in your neighborhood or workplace? And help others do the same?

Personal Growth Plan

Which **SMART objective(s)** will you pursue this week?

_____

_____

_____

For Daily Prayer

Holy Spirit, thank You for Your presence in my life. Infuse me with the light of Christ so that I might willingly shine for Him and witness to His great mercy and grace. Give me the courage to share with others what You have done in my life. In Jesus' name. Amen.

– Kindling the Heart of the Christ-like Servant Leader, 3rd Edition (page 28)

Daily Bible Reflections: Day 1

Read and Highlight: Matthew 5:13-16

Words or phrases that catch my attention:

_____
_____
_____

Major Thought:

_____

What impresses me the most, and what I'll do about it:

_____
_____
_____

What does this Scripture lead me to pray about? (This may be praise and thanks; or with apology, asking forgiveness and help; or a request for wisdom, or for some other need.)

_____
_____

Daily Bible Reflections: Day 2

Date: ___ /___ /___

Read and Highlight: Colossians 4:5-6

Words or phrases that catch my attention:

_____
_____
_____

Major Thought:

_____

What impresses me the most, and what I'll do about it:

_____
_____
_____

What does this Scripture lead me to pray about?

_____
_____

Daily Bible Reflections: Day 3

Date: __ / __ / __

Read and Highlight: Matthew 28:16–20

Words or phrases that catch my attention:

_____

_____

_____

Major Thought:

_____

What impresses me the most, and what I'll do about it:

_____

_____

_____

What does this Scripture lead me to pray about?

_____

_____

Daily Bible Reflections: Day 4

Date: __ / __ / __

Read and Highlight: Acts 17:22–33

Words or phrases that catch my attention:

_____

_____

_____

Major Thought:

_____

What impresses me the most, and what I'll do about it:

_____

_____

_____

What does this Scripture lead me to pray about?

_____

_____

Daily Bible Reflections: Day 5

Read and Highlight: Matthew 13:1-9, 18-23

Words or phrases that catch my attention:

_____

_____

_____

Major Thought:

_____

What impresses me the most, and what I'll do about it:

_____

_____

_____

What does this Scripture lead me to pray about?

_____

_____

Daily Bible Reflections: Day 6

Date: ___ /___ /___

Review the passages you reflected on this week.

Which reading(s) spoke most directly to you this week?

_____

_____

_____

What is God saying to you in this reading?

_____

_____

_____

How are you responding?

_____

_____

_____

Prepare for The Christ-like Servant Leader Cluster Meeting by reviewing the Agenda on the next page and considering your responses.

Christ-like Servant Leader Cluster Meeting 6

Opening Prayer

Pray together, or ask for a volunteer to pray the following prayer:

Lord Jesus, Your continual witness to the Father's ever-present love is amazing and inspiring. Your life was a testimony to obedience, well-being, leadership, and community. Your words and life continually teach us how to live as God's dearly loved children today. Help us to be Your faithful witnesses wherever we find ourselves. In Your name, we pray. Amen.

Discussion Questions:

1. What do you think of when you hear the word "witness" or "evangelism?

2. Which of the five Scripture readings this week has been particularly meaningful to you? What has God been saying to you through it? How are you responding?

3. How is daily time in Scripture shaping and empowering you as a willing and ready witness?

4. What's one way you can be a voice and example of God's restoring grace and mercy in your congregation, family, neighborhood or workplace this week? How can you help others do the same?

5. What **SMART Objective** needs your attention this week? What so you need to happen to make positive progress?

Closing Prayer

Let's take time to do two things:

1. Write down prayer requests:
   a. As we pray for each other this week, what is one thing can we pray for you?

   b. As we learn and live out the practice *Witness Willingly*, what are we led to pray?

2. Pray together, focusing on the needs identified in number 1.

Serve Others
Daily Reflections from God's Word for Week 7

Remembering Who We Are

A KINDLE Christ-like servant leader helps others:

- Celebrate their Baptismal identity (restored, gifted, called);
- Grow more Christ-like, manifesting the Grace-Filled Marks of obedience, well-being, leadership, and community; and
- Foster and multiply generations of Christ-like servant leaders in their congregations, homes, workplaces, communities, and the world.

This Week's Focus: Practice 1.5 — Serve Others

Go forth as a living sacrifice, being God's ambassador of reconciliation to all people, especially to the least of these.

- *Knowledge — Recognize that serving others is part of God's restoring and reconciling work in the world.*
- *Skill — Serve others by practicing hospitality, showing mercy, and doing justice.*
- *Attitude — Open your heart generously, as Jesus did, when you serve others.*

Core Concept

The Christ-like servant leader is a servant first. As he/she addresses the needs of others, the role of leader naturally emerges.

Now What?

As you interact with God's Word this week, pay attention to who Jesus is, what He does, and the example He sets for us. What do you notice about the place of boasting?

Personal Growth Plan

After six weeks of pursuing your growth plan, how are you feeling about it? Which **SMART objective(s)** do you need to be focusing on this week?

_____

_____

_____

For Daily Prayer

Gracious Heavenly Father, when I reflect on the ways You provide for everything I need, I am overwhelmed and grateful. Let my gratitude move me to see the hurting and hungry in a new way. Increase my willingness and my capacity to respond to Your provision by serving the needs of others. I am honored and humbled to do so. In Jesus' name. Amen.

– Kindling the Heart of the Christ-like Servant Leader, 3rd Edition (page 29)

Daily Bible Reflections: Day 1

Read and Highlight: 1 Peter 4:8-11

Words or phrases that catch my attention:

_____

_____

_____

Major Thought:

_____

What impresses me the most, and what I'll do about it:

_____

_____

_____

What does this Scripture lead me to pray about? (This may be praise and thanks; or with apology, asking forgiveness and help; or a request for wisdom, or for some other need.)

_____

_____

Daily Bible Reflections: Day 2

Date: ___ /___ /___

Read and Highlight: Galatians 5:13-15

Words or phrases that catch my attention:

_____

_____

_____

Major Thought:

_____

What impresses me the most, and what I'll do about it:

_____

_____

_____

What does this Scripture lead me to pray about?

_____

_____

Daily Bible Reflections: Day 3

Date: ___ /___ /___

Read and Highlight: Matthew 25:31–40

Words or phrases that catch my attention:

_____

_____

_____

Major Thought:

_____

What impresses me the most, and what I'll do about it:

_____

_____

_____

What does this Scripture lead me to pray about?

_____

_____

Daily Bible Reflections: Day 4

Date: ___ /___ /___

Read and Highlight: Ephesians 2:8–10

Words or phrases that catch my attention:

_____

_____

Major Thought:

_____

What impresses me the most, and what I'll do about it:

_____

_____

What does this Scripture lead me to pray about?

_____

_____

Daily Bible Reflections: Day 5

Date: ___ / ___ / ___

Read and Highlight: Philippians 2:1-11

Words or phrases that catch my attention:

_____

_____

_____

Major Thought:

_____

What impresses me the most, and what I'll do about it:

_____

_____

_____

What does this Scripture lead me to pray about?

_____

_____

Daily Bible Reflections: Day 6

Date: ___ / ___ / ___

Review the passages you reflected on this week.

Which reading(s) spoke most directly to you this week?

_____

_____

_____

What is God saying to you in this reading?

_____

_____

_____

How are you responding?

_____

_____

_____

Prepare for The Christ-like Servant Leader Cluster Meeting by reviewing the Agenda on the next page and considering your responses.

Christ-like Servant Leader Cluster Meeting 7 Date: ___ /___ /___

Opening Prayer

Pray together, or ask for a volunteer to pray the following prayer:

Lord Jesus, forgive our foolish ways and times we seek to be served rather than to serve. Imprint Your life on us and help us practice Your example and live as an ambassador of Your restoring and reconciling work in the world. Amen.

Discussion Questions:

1. Share a time when someone really served you in an unexpected way. How about a time you served someone?

2. Which of the five Scripture readings this week has been particularly meaningful to you? What has God been saying to you through it? How are you responding?

3. What's the place of boasting in the life of a Christ-like servant leader?

4. Consider the needs of people around you. Who might God be inviting you to serve this week, and how?

5. Where in your growth plan are you still investing energy? What is going well?

Closing Prayer

Let's take time to do two things:

1. Write down prayer requests:
   a. As we pray for each other this week, what is one thing can we pray for you?

   b. As we learn and live out the practice *Serve Others*, what are we led to pray?

2. Pray together, focusing on the needs identified in number 1.

Reviewing the 5 Practices
Daily Reflections from God's Word for Week 8

Remembering Who We Are

A KINDLE Christ-like servant leader helps others:

- Celebrate their Baptismal identity (restored, gifted, called);
- Grow more Christ-like, manifesting the Grace-Filled Marks of obedience, well-being, leadership, and community; and
- Foster and multiply generations of Christ-like servant leaders in their congregations, homes, workplaces, communities, and the world.

This Week's Focus: Reviewing the 5 Practices

1. *Embrace Sabbath Living* – Eagerly worship, partake in Holy Communion, and nurture additional behaviors which foster spiritual renewal and rest.
2. *Learn and Live Scripture* – Discover and apply the truths of Scripture in all your comings and goings.
3. *Pray Unceasingly* – Pray continually – alone and with others – for all people, the church, and the world.
4. *Witness Willingly* – Accept God's call to be a voice and example of His restoring grace and mercy in your communities and in the world.
5. *Serve Others* – Go forth as a living sacrifice, being God's ambassador of reconciliation to all people, especially to the least of these.

Core Concept

Christ-like servant leaders continually attend to the practices that cultivate a living faith in the context of community and help others do the same.

Now What?

Through these practices, God transforms, equips, and empowers our living in Christ, as Christ-like Servant Leaders. In what ways has the Journey of Cultivating Faith impacted your life? How might you continue to cultivate these practices? Might it include continuing with your KINDLE cluster into Cultivating Health? How about inviting others to join you on this Journey of Cultivating Faith?

Personal Growth Plan

As you reflect on your Growth Plan efforts over the last seven weeks, what results are you pleased with? Which **SMART objectives** can you still pursue this week and beyond?

_____

_____

_____

Complete the Christ-like Servant Leader Evaluation on pages 45–46.

For Daily Prayer

Heavenly Father, I thank You for the many times Your Spirit has enriched my conversations with You. Such times are a true gift and keep me healthy and hopeful. Forgive me when I try to go it alone. Provide me the courage to keep seeking conversation and consolation with others. In Jesus' name. Amen.

– Kindling the Heart of the Christ-like Servant Leader, 3rd Edition (page 35)

Daily Bible Reflections: Day 1

Date: ___ /___ /___

Read and Highlight: Isaiah 40:28-31

Words or phrases that catch my attention:

_____

_____

_____

Major Thought:

_____

What impresses me the most, and what I'll do about it:

_____

_____

_____

What does this Scripture lead me to pray about? (This may be praise and thanks; or with apology, asking forgiveness and help; or a request for wisdom, or for some other need.)

_____

_____

Daily Bible Reflections: Day 2

Date: ___ /___ /___

Read and Highlight: Psalm 119:33-40

Words or phrases that catch my attention:

_____

_____

_____

Major Thought:

_____

What impresses me the most, and what I'll do about it:

_____

_____

_____

What does this Scripture lead me to pray about?

_____

_____

Daily Bible Reflections: Day 3

Date: __ /__ /__

Read and Highlight: Colossians 1:3-12

Words or phrases that catch my attention:

_____

_____

_____

Major Thought:

_____

What impresses me the most, and what I'll do about it:

_____

_____

_____

What does this Scripture lead me to pray about?

_____

_____

Daily Bible Reflections: Day 4

Date: __ /__ /__

Read and Highlight: 1 Peter 2:9-10

Words or phrases that catch my attention:

_____

_____

_____

Major Thought:

_____

What impresses me the most, and what I'll do about it:

_____

_____

_____

What does this Scripture lead me to pray about?

_____

_____

Daily Bible Reflections: Day 5

Date: __ /__ /__

Read and Highlight: Galatians 6:1-10

Words or phrases that catch my attention:

_____
_____
_____

Major Thought:

_____

What impresses me the most, and what I'll do about it:

_____
_____
_____

What does this Scripture lead me to pray about?

_____
_____

Daily Bible Reflections: Day 6

Date: __ /__ /__

Review the passages you reflected on this week.

Which reading(s) spoke most directly to you this week?

_____
_____
_____

What is God saying to you in this reading?

_____
_____
_____

How are you responding?

_____
_____
_____

*Please note special instructions on page 44 as you prepare for
the Christ-like Servant Leader Cluster Meeting.*

Prepare for The Servant Leader Cluster Meeting by completing the evaluation and reviewing the Agenda on the following pages. Bring the completed evaluation to the next meeting. Your feedback is important to KINDLE as we continue to refine this material.

Christ-like Servant Leader Journey Evaluation — Cultivating Faith

Name: _____   Date: _____

Your ministry staff is delighted you participated in an 8-week KINDLE cluster. As part of our commitment to a quality KINDLE experience, you're being asked to complete this short evaluation form. As you do so, please be aware that your responses will be viewed by the following individuals: your cluster leader, your KINDLE Associate, and Senior Pastor. We deeply appreciate your taking the time to complete this evaluation.

Yours and other cluster member responses will also be shared with KINDLE's Executive Leadership Team and Board of Directors in aggregate form. No names will be attached to your responses.

Impact On You as a Christ-like Servant Leader

Please rate your reaction to the following statements using a scale from 1 *(very little impact)* to 6 *(very significant impact)*. Include any comments you may have after each question.

1. **Describe the impact this cluster experience has had on Christ-like servant leadership in your life.**

   Scale: 1 *(very little impact)* to 6 *(very significant impact)*

   _____ My **understanding of what it means to be** a Christ-like servant leader.
   Comments:

   _____ My **view of myself as** a Christ-like servant leader.
   Comments:

   _____ My **commitment to be** a Christ-like servant leader.
   Comments:

   _____ My **desire to equip others to be** Christ-like servant leaders.
   Comments:

   _____ My **overall capacity to be** a Christ-like servant leader.
   Comments:

2. **How has your cluster experience helped you "live out" each of the five practices of Cultivating Faith?**

   Scale: 1 *(less evidence of practice)* to 6 *(more evidence)*

   _____ Embrace Sabbath Living
   Comments:

   _____ Learn and Live Scripture
   Comments:

   _____ Pray Unceasingly
   Comments:

   _____ Witness Willingly
   Comments:

   _____ Serve Others
   Comments:

Christ-like Servant Leader Journey Evaluation — Cultivating Faith

3. As a result of my being in this Christ-like servant leader experience, my life is different in the following ways:

_____

_____

_____

_____

_____

_____

4. As a result of my being in this Christ-like servant leader experience, I have taken on the following new leadership roles in my home, workplace, congregation, community, and beyond (please feel free to add 2-3 examples)…

_____

_____

_____

_____

_____

_____

5. As a result of my being in this Christ-like servant leader cluster, **my sense of ministry as a Christ-like servant leader is…**

Circle one:

Unfocused / Beginning to be more focused / Somewhat focused / More focused / Much more focused / Laser focused

Please share any additional thoughts, ideas, comments, or suggestions:

_____

_____

_____

_____

_____

Thank you for sharing your honest feedback!
Please bring this completed evaluation to your week 8 cluster meeting.

Christ-like Servant Leader Cluster Meeting 8   Date: __ / __ / __

Opening Prayer

Pray together, or ask for a volunteer to pray the following prayer:

Thank you for our KINDLE Journey, Lord, and for helping us begin to see who we are as baptized children of God: united with You and called to be like You! Apart from You, that's impossible. Give us the grace to integrate and engage these practices in our lives – not as an external code, but as a way to stay connected to You. In Jesus' name, we pray. Amen.

Discussion Questions:

1. In what ways has this *Journey of Cultivating Faith* impacted your life?

2. Which of the five Scripture readings this week has been particularly meaningful to you? What has God been saying to you through it? How are you responding?

3. How might you continue to cultivate these five practices? Might it include continuing with your KINDLE cluster into *Cultivating Health*? Or inviting others to join you on this *Journey of Cultivating Faith*?

4. Who can you share the Gospel with this week in word and action?

5. After seven weeks, how are you doing with your growth plan? In what ways has it enhanced your capacity as a Christ-like servant leader? Do you still have more **SMART objectives** you'd like to pursue? Or are you ready for a new plan? Or a break?

6. We're blessed to be a blessing! In what way(s) has each person in this cluster blessed your cluster experience?

Closing Prayer

Let's take time to do two things:

1. Write down prayer requests:
   a. As we pray for each other this week, what is one thing can we pray for you?

   b. As we learn and live out the five practices that *Cultivate Faith*, what prayer is needed?

2. Pray together, giving thanks for this Journey and each other, focusing on the needs identified in number 1.

What Is My Baptismal Identity?

Restored!

Apart from Christ and not knowing Him, we live as enemies of God. In the waters of Baptism, God justifies us by his generous grace! "Justify" is a legal term that declares us innocent in the face of evidence to the contrary. We are adopted into His family and are heirs of eternal life. This frees us from trying to earn God's approval or our salvation. We're given a new beginning and filled with the Holy Spirit so we can become more like Jesus, devoting ourselves to the good He would do. (Titus 3:3-8)

Gifted!

Christ gives gifts to His people "in order to prepare God's people to serve and to build up the body of Christ. This is to continue until all of us are united in our faith and in our knowledge about God's Son, until we become mature, until we measure up to Christ, who is the standard." (Ephesians 4:12-13 GW) Each believer is given at least one gift to put to use in serving others. To discover more and consider what yours might be, read 1 Corinthians 12, Ephesians 4:7-16, and Romans 12:3-8.

Called!

As part of God's family, we're called to reflect our status as His beloved daughters and sons. You are clothed with Christ (Galatians 3:27), and called to "throw off your old sinful nature and your former way of life, which is corrupted by lust and deception. Instead, let the Spirit renew your thoughts and attitudes. Put on your new nature, created to be like God—truly righteous and holy." (Ephesians 4:22-24 NLT)

KINDLE Christ-like servant leaders are in an ongoing, lifetime journey of becoming who God declares us to be in the waters of Baptism and helping others do the same! Enjoy the journey!

Notes for Leaders and Apprentices as They Begin a Christ-like Servant Leader Journey Cluster

Rationale for the Christ-like Servant Leader Journey Cluster Experience

The *Christ-like Servant Leader Journey* is designed to deepen a person's understanding of, and commitment to, Christ-like servant leadership. The *Christ-like Servant Leader Journey* is a part of a *Christ-like Servant Leader Development Process* (see page 51) that results in individuals being deployed into their congregation, home, work place, and community to foster and multiply Christ-like servant leaders.

The *Christ-like Servant Leader Journey* is also designed to be used in a Cluster of one leader plus 3-4 members. The idea stems from Ecclesiastes 4:12 – "One person could be overpowered. But two people can stand up for themselves. And a rope made out of three cords isn't easily broken." (NIRV) Christ-like Servant Leader Clusters are designed to be strong enough to provide support, encouragement, and accountability; but flexible enough to work around members' busy schedules.

Steps to Forming a Cluster

Step # 1 – Identify: Look for the Christ-like servant leader potential in everyone and help them recognize it.

The first step is to identify potential members for your *Christ-like Servant Leader Journey Cluster*. Begin by asking the "Lord of the harvest" (Luke 10:2) to bring names of potential members to mind. Write a list. Keep praying for those on the list. Seek counsel from others on your team.

Step # 2 – Invite: Invite people to engage in the Christ-like Servant Leader Journey.

Inviting is a simple task that is often hard to do. Why? When we invite people, we are stepping outside of our known relational comfort zone. We may think we need to "sell" the opportunity and convince people to say "yes" to something they wouldn't want to do. Not knowing how the person will respond—and the fear of a negative response—often keeps us from attempting to make a connection. Prayerfully consider how you've experienced the Journey, its value to you, and how you've been blessed. Invite people into the blessing. Those God intends to bring together will be available and say, "yes!" If you receive a "no," for whatever reason, do not take it personally. There may be another time when the person will say "yes."

A few tips as you invite…

- Timing and place are important. While you'll be tempted to do the inviting on Sunday morning because it's so convenient, resist! It's worth both the time and effort to do the inviting in a much less pressured and rushed environment.
- Always be honest. Share how the Journey has impacted you. Be clear about the expectations and the time and tasks involved. Don't undersell, yet affirm that it's worth it.
- Share the vision. Help people see the "bigger picture." "Vision without a task is only a dream. A task without a vision is but drudgery. But vision with a task is a dream fulfilled."
- ICNU … What do you see in people? Encourage and affirm their gifts.

Getting Ready for the First Meeting

Here are some tips for getting ready for your first meeting:

1. Consider meeting in a coffee shop, restaurant, or park. You'd be surprised who'll be watching!
2. Connect personally with every group member prior to the meeting. Give them the details of the group. Make sure they know when and where you'll be meeting. Give them something in writing!
3. Become familiar with the major components of the first meeting and envision your use of time.
   a. (15 minutes) Orientation to KINDLE, Christ-like servant leadership, and the Journey Guide (pages 1-2)
   b. (15 minutes) Our Journey Begins (page 3)
   c. (15 minutes) Developing a Personal Growth Plan (pages 4-5)
   d. (5 minutes) Closing – preview of next week's assignment (pages 5, 10)
   e. (10 minutes) Prayer time (page 5)
   f. If you think the meeting may go a little longer than 60 minutes, say so upfront and check availability.
4. Take care of all the details regarding the environment – i.e., the room, time, lighting, etc.
5. Be there early to welcome everyone and introduce people to each other.
6. Pray that all who attend will connect with one another and be blessed by the process.
7. Relax and be yourself as you lead, encouraging all to open their hearts and minds.

Importance of Preparing Each Week

The best group experience flows from being adequately prepared. Please promise yourself that you will do so. Full engage the daily journey for yourself and let God work in you. Pray for those in your cluster. Listen for where God is at work and give thanks. Watch for signs of readiness in others to facilitate portions of the Cluster Meeting. Be ready to encourage and build up others on the journey, and to be encouraged and built up!

Recruit and develop others as apprentice leaders using a simple, straightforward process.

A helpful practice is to always invite someone to join you as an apprentice in every ministry journey. Why is this important? Developing apprentice leaders sets in motion a potential leadership development pipeline. Paul speaks of reproducing leaders into the fourth generation. He instructs Timothy to invest in "reliable men" who will also be qualified to develop others: "You have heard me teach things that have been confirmed by many reliable witnesses. Now teach these truths to other trustworthy people who will be able to pass them on to others." (2 Timothy 2:2 NLT)

1st Generation: Paul
2nd Generation: Timothy
3rd Generation: Trustworthy people
4th Generation: To others

An apprentice is someone who is learning to lead … by leading! Apprentices are different than assistants, co-leaders, and helpers. The difference is that the apprentice is not simply helping a leader; rather, the apprentice is in the process of becoming a leader. Little by little, topic by topic, over time, on the job.

Christ-like servant leaders apprentice people in different ways. For example, God leads some to invite cluster members to grow together through several Journey Guides. These leaders invite any or all of the cluster members to lead portions of the weekly cluster meetings as they see gifts, abilities, or readiness to do so. Over time, these leaders also plant seeds of possibility: "Look at the impact God is making in your life. Who in your network is at the place where you started when this Journey began? What if you could invite them into your own cluster?"

Normally, though, Christ-like servant leaders are led to identify an apprentice leader before the first cluster meeting and intentionally develop them over the eight weeks of this Journey Guide. These leaders will find the five step apprenticing model to be a very helpful, practical way of developing apprentice leaders.

Five Step Apprenticing Model

1. I do. You watch. We talk.
2. I do. You help. We talk.
3. You do. I help. We talk.
4. You do. I watch. We talk.
5. You do. Someone else watches you. I find a new apprentice who watches … and so on!

Cultivating Faith

1. *Embrace Sabbath Living*
2. *Learn and Live Scripture*
3. *Pray Unceasingly*
4. *Witness Willingly*
5. *Serve Others*

Grace-filled Mark:
Obedience

Cultivating Health

1. *Recognize God's Call*
2. *Pursue Wellness*
3. *Grow in Wisdom*
4. *Optimize Finances*
5. *Stay Connected*

Grace-filled Mark:
Well-being

Cultivating Individuals

1. *Set the Example*
2. *Voice the Vision*
3. *Equip to Multiply*
4. *Spur One Another*
5. *Encourage One Another*

Grace-filled Mark:
Leadership

Cultivating Groups

1. *Build the Community*
2. *Identify Common Vision*
3. *Promote Communication*
4. *Manage Anxiety and Conflict*
5. *Nurture Collaboration*

Grace-filled Mark:
Community

Christ-like Servant Leadership
Strands and Practices Overview

There are four main strands, or components, in this model that are designed to strengthen our understanding of and commitment to being a Christ-like servant leader wherever we are. Each strand has a set of five practices that are defining behaviors of a Christ-like servant leader. An 8-week Christ-Like Servant Leader Journey Guide has been developed for each strand and serves as one tool for growing as a Christ-like servant leader.

KINDLE
Fostering & Multiplying Christ-like Servant Leaders

KINDLEServantLeaders.org

Made in the USA
Las Vegas, NV
09 December 2021

36808070R00032